# by Chloe Perkins
## illustrated by Tom Woolley

READY-TO-READ

SIMON SPOTLIGHT

An imprint of Simon & Schuster Children's Publishing Division • New York  London  Toronto  Sydney  New Delhi • 1230 Avenue of the Americas, New York, New York 10020 • This Simon Spotlight edition October 2016 • Text copyright © 2016 by Simon & Schuster, Inc. Illustrations copyright © 2016 by Tom Woolley • All rights reserved, including the right of reproduction in whole or in part in any form. SIMON SPOTLIGHT, READY-TO-READ, and colophon are registered trademarks of Simon & Schuster, Inc. For information about special discounts for bulk purchases, please contact Simon & Schuster Special Sales at 1-866-506-1949 or business@simonandschuster.com. Manufactured in the United States of America 0721 LAK  6  8  10  9  7  5
Library of Congress Cataloging-in-Publication Data
Names: Perkins, Chloe, author. | Woolley, Tom, 1981- illustrator. Title: Living in . . . South Africa / by Chloe Perkins ; illustrated by Tom Woolley. Other titles: South Africa | Living in . . . (Simon and Schuster, Inc.) Description: New York : Simon & Schuster, 2016. | Series: Living in . . . | "Simon spotlight." Identifiers: LCCN 2016008603 | ISBN 9781481470926 (trade paper) | ISBN 9781481470933 (hardcover) | ISBN 9781481470940 (eBook) Subjects: LCSH: South Africa—Juvenile literature. | South Africa—Social life and customs—Juvenile literature. Classification: LCC DT1719 .P465 2016 | DDC 968—dc23 LC record available at http://lccn.loc.gov/2016008603

# GLOSSARY

**Afrikaans:** a language spoken in South Africa that is based on Dutch

**Ancestor:** a family member who lived a long time ago

**Basin:** a low area of land into which bodies of water flow

**Coast:** land that touches a large body of water

**Descendant:** someone related to a person or group of people who lived a long time ago

**Election:** an event in which people vote for their leaders

**Grassland:** a large area of land covered by grass and small plants

**Homelands:** poor, crowded areas where many nonwhite South Africans were forced to live during apartheid

**Northern Sotho:** a language spoken in South Africa that is part of the Bantu language family

**Plateau:** a flat area of land that is raised higher than the land around it

**Protest:** an action or statement made by a person to show that he or she disagrees with something

**Resist:** to fight against or refuse to accept something

**Rugby:** a popular sport in South Africa that is similar to American football

**Tribe:** a group of people who share the same language and culture

**Xhosa:** a people who live mainly in South Africa; also a language spoken in South Africa that is part of the Bantu language family

**Zulu:** a people who live mainly in South Africa; also the most widely spoken language in South Africa; the language is part of the Bantu language family

**NOTE TO READERS:** Some of these words may have more than one definition. The definitions above are how these words are used in this book.

*Dumela!* (say: doo-MEL-ah) That means "hi" in Northern Sotho (say: SOO-too). My name is David, and I live in South Africa. South Africa is a country in Africa where more than fifty million people live . . . including me!

South Africa is on the southern tip of Africa. It borders six countries. One of those countries, Lesotho (say: leh-SOO-too), is within South Africa's borders!

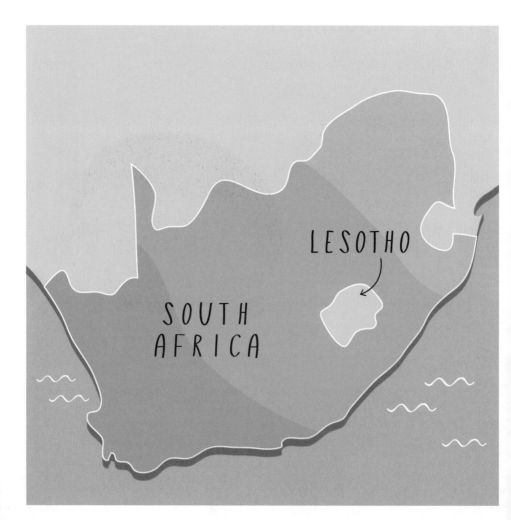

Much of South Africa is covered by plateaus (say: pla-TOES), which are tall, flat areas of land. The plateaus have grasslands on top.
Lots of animals, like rhinos, zebras, cheetahs, lions, and elephants live in the grasslands.

Above the plateaus, the land
dips down to form the
Kalahari (say: kah-lah-HAH-ree)
Basin. Some parts of the basin
are a sandy desert,
while other parts are grassy.

Along the coast is the Great Escarpment, where the plateaus drop off. Drakensberg is a very tall mountain range along the eastern part of the Great Escarpment. In the Afrikaans language, Drakensberg means "mountains of dragons"!

A very famous South African,
Archbishop Desmond Tutu, called
South Africa the "rainbow nation."
That's because South Africans come
from many different cultures.
Lots of people are descendants
of African tribes like the
Xhosa (say: K-OH-sah) and Zulu.

Some people trace their origins to India. Their ancestors may have come to South Africa as slaves or laborers hundreds of years ago. Others are descendants of Europeans who came from Holland, France, and England. Whatever our heritage, today we are all South Africans.

**JOHANNESBURG**

South Africa has many big cities. Johannesburg was founded during a gold rush. A theme park was later built around one of the gold mines! Cape Town sits in the shadow of Table Mountain, a flat-topped mountain that looks down on the city.

**CAPE TOWN**

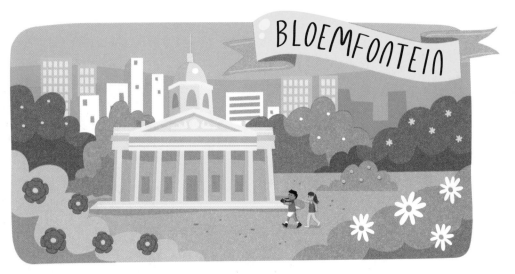

Bloemfontein (say: BLOOM-fohn-tane) is known as the city of roses. Its name means "fountain of flowers" in Dutch! Pretoria is home to the biggest zoo in South Africa. It houses many of the coolest plants and animals in our country!

PRETORIA

I live in a house in a suburb
of Pretoria with my mom,
dad, older sister, and
older brother.

My dad is a software engineer.
He creates programs for computers.
My mom is an accountant.
She helps people with their money.
My sister wants to be a doctor
when she grows up. My brother
plays a sport called rugby.

We get up really early each
morning—around five thirty!
After I get dressed in my
school uniform, I have
breakfast with my family.
We usually eat cereal or
porridge.

Because my brother, sister,
and I go to a private school
in the city, we have a long
bus trip. We take our first
bus to downtown Pretoria
and our second bus to another
neighborhood where our school is.
The trip takes a little over an hour.

School starts at 7:45 a.m. There are thirty students in my class. Each day is split into eight different sections, or periods. We learn languages, math, science, music, gym, geography, and history. Our first lesson is history.

We have been learning about
apartheid (say: ah-PAR-tate).
Apartheid was a time in our
history when the government
discriminated against people
of color. It began in 1948,
when a group called the
National Party won the election.

The National Party believed
that white people were better
than people of other races.
They forced anyone who wasn't
white to carry papers if
they wanted to travel outside
certain areas. Anyone caught
without their papers was arrested.

As time went on, things only
got worse. More than three million
people were forced to give up
their homes and land to the
government, which then resold
the land to white people. People
of other races were forced into poor,
crowded areas called "homelands."

People of other races who lived
outside the homelands were
separated from white South Africans
in schools, theaters, and
restaurants. On top of everything,
the government stripped nonwhite
people of their right to vote.

Many South Africans resisted
apartheid, joining groups such as
the African National Congress (ANC).
Among the ANC's leaders was
a lawyer named Nelson Mandela.
Mandela organized protests and told
people to fight apartheid laws.
He was arrested for his beliefs.

Even though he was in jail, Mandela became a symbol for the resistance. By 1989, protests and demands from the people, as well as pressure from countries around the world, started to bring apartheid to an end. Nelson Mandela was released from prison in 1990.

In 1994, South Africans of every race were able to vote in the new elections. Nelson Mandela won the election to become South Africa's first black president!

After our history lesson, we have languages. We learn English and Northern Sotho, but South Africa has eleven official languages in all! Some of the other official languages include Xhosa, Zulu, and Afrikaans.

After English, we work on our math lesson and then head to lunch. I usually pack a lunch from home, but today is Wednesday. That means it's macaroni and cheese day! I always eat a school lunch on Wednesdays.

After lunch we have lessons in geography and then science. In science we are learning about archaeology (say: ark-ay-AHL-oh-jee), or the study of how people in the past lived. There are many fossils and ancient cave paintings to study in South Africa!

Next we have music and gym class, and then school is over. My brother, sister, and I meet to walk to the bus stop. Once we get home, my sister helps me with my homework. Then I play a computer game.

When my parents get home,
we go outside to play rugby.
Rugby is a sport similar
to American football. My brother
and I have played rugby in
summer programs. Rugby is
one of the most popular sports
in South Africa.

During apartheid, rugby was mostly played by white South Africans while black South Africans played soccer. But after apartheid ended and we won the Rugby World Cup in 1995, black South Africans were urged to play rugby as well. Today, rugby is a popular sport among many people.

Dinnertime! We're having samp, or crushed corn, and beans with sheep tripe. Tripe means "stomach." It's really tasty! After dinner I help my big brother clean up and do a few chores before bed.

On some nights my family and I
stay up watching rugby.
Our team plays against countries
from all around the world!
Someday I'm going to visit all
those countries to see their rugby
teams play. Would you like to visit
South Africa someday?

# ALL ABOUT
# SOUTH AFRICA!

**NAME:** Republic of South Africa (or South Africa for short!)

**POPULATION:** 53 million

**CAPITAL:** South Africa has three capitals! Bloemfontein is the capital for the courts, Cape Town is the capital for lawmaking, and Pretoria is the administrative capital, where the president lives.

**LANGUAGE:** South Africa has eleven official languages, but the most spoken languages are Zulu, Xhosa, Afrikaans, and English.

**TOTAL AREA:** 470,693 square miles

**GOVERNMENT:** republic

**CURRENCY:** rand

**FUN FACT:** South Africa is rich in minerals—it produces the most platinum in the world, and is a leading producer of diamonds, coal, and gold. The largest white diamond in the world, the Cullinan Diamond, was found near Pretoria, South Africa, in 1905.

**FLAG:** Two equal bands of red and blue separated by a central green band that forms a sideways *Y*. A black triangle to the left of the *Y* is outlined by thin yellow bands.